MENTAL TOUGHNESS TRAINING PROGRAM

The Ultimate Guide To Develop A Growth Mindset To Gain More Happiness, Self Esteem, Wealth And Freedom In Life And Live A Happy Life

By Roman Power

Mental Toughness Training Program

Table of Contents

INTRODUCTION 8

CHAPTER 1: HOW TO DEVELOP REASONING SKILLS? 10

DEDUCTIVE REASONING 10

INDUCTIVE REASONING 11

ABDUCTIVE REASONING 12

RETRODUCTIVE REASONING 13

CRITICAL THINKING IN TEXTUAL ANALYSIS 14

    Read the material analytically 15

    Think critically 15

    Be objective 16

    Recognize the structure of the message 17

    Draw your inference 17

    Raise queries and challenges 18

HOW YOU APPLY SOUND REASONING AND TEXTUAL ANALYSIS 19

    Verify claims before concluding 20

    Entertain differing opinions 21

    Evaluate the implications of your held perspective 21

    Resolve your differences with logic and evidence 22

    Be open to change 22

CHAPTER 2: MIND MAPPING 24

WHAT DO YOU USE MIND MAPPING FOR? 28

BENEFITS AND PROGRAMS 34

CHAPTER 3: ANALYSIS TECHNIQUES 36

BRAINSTORMING 36

    Brainstorming meetings: 36

    Effective Brainstorming Session: 37

The Hybrid model: *38*

Rules for Brainstorming: *39*

Mind Storming *40*

The Pareto Principle *41*

80/20 Rule in life *41*

CHAPTER 4: BENEFITS OF CRITICAL THINKING 46

ONE SIDE OF THE COIN: 5 ADVANTAGES OF CRITICAL THINKING 46

THE FLIP SIDE TO THE COIN: 5 DISADVANTAGES OF CRITICAL THINKING 49

EVALUATING PATTERNS OF THINKING 55

CHAPTER 5: TYPES OF CRITICAL THINKING 60

LOGICAL REASONING 60

SCIENTIFIC REASONING 62

THE PSYCHOLOGY OF CRITICAL THINKING 63

PRACTICAL DOMAIN 64

THEORETICAL DOMAIN 65

METHODOLOGICAL DOMAIN 66

FOUR GOALS FOR CRITICAL THINKING 68

Self-Direction *68*

Self-Discipline *68*

Self-Monitoring *69*

Self-Correction *69*

CHAPTER 5: WHEN TO APPLY CRITICAL THINKING TO IMPROVE

SOMETHING 72

THE TAKEAWAY 79

Reason why some people have a tough time with critical thinking *79*

How Do People Struggle with Critical Thinking? *80*

It's Very Hard for Many People to Let Go of Biases and Prejudices *81*

A Lot of People are Mentally Uncomfortable with Critical Thinking *82*

How to Be a Critical Thinker Using These 7 Techniques *83*

CHAPTER 6: BEST PRACTICE FOR IMPROVING CRITICAL THINKING SKILLS 86

Take A Breath, and Have a Thought 86

Practice Careful Reading and Synthesis of Information 86

Talk to Yourself 87

Break Down a Task into Its Parts 87

Give Yourself a Real Goal 88

Know Thy Adversary 89

The Martian Tourist 90

Sample Process 97

CONCLUSION 100

Introduction

When you learn how to think critically, you are able to better understand the world around you. You are able to examine any tidbit of information that comes your way in a way that is unbiased, informed, and practical in order to determine whether it is trustworthy or biased, and in developing this ability, you can decipher between something being a valid thought, belief, or assertion.

Stop and consider when this may be useful—you may use critical thinking skills to parse between real and fake news. You may use it to understand if the person that has been talking to you seems like they may be lying about something or if they are worthy of your focus. When you can think critically, you can start to problem-solve—you can see what is right or wrong, or you can figure out how to prioritize the importance of what you have on your to-do list. It extends throughout several aspects of your life, and when you are able to come up with solid critical thinking skills, you will find that you are able to make good, reasonable judgments based on the information that you have been provided, as well as able to take out any information that does not matter to you.

By being a good critical thinker and mastering the skills you will learn as you read, you will become a more active learner and be in control of how much information you absorb. This is an essential skill for students in all different fields. You will also become more empathetic because you will grow to understand all different viewpoints and backgrounds.

The following will break down what critical thinking means and what you must have to achieve it. This guide will provide you with diagrams and explanations that will appeal to all different types of learners. You will learn how to eliminate bias in your everyday life to become an efficient problem solver. This will also help you understand where biases are present in your life. This guide utilizes real-life examples that will allow you to relate to the content.

It will further teach you how to train your brain to react to different situations, first by allowing you to understand how your brain functions.

Lastly, you will learn a few strategies to increase how much you think critically in your everyday life.

Chapter 1:
How to Develop Reasoning Skills?

In life, you will interact with other people when it comes to communication and exchanging ideas. At various times, you may differ with or agree with each other. Most often, your position on a given topic will depend on your innate preconceptions and beliefs. However, to develop as critical thinking, you do not just have to follow convention based on their face value. You could improve your critical thinking skills by evaluating said ideas and eliminating bias in your inferences. As a result, you intelligently choose what to accept and believe, and discard useless assumptions.

Therefore, apply the following reasoning methods to your various situations as and when needed:

Deductive Reasoning

Being an expert on deductive reasoning will require you to pay special attention to the premise of a given conclusion. Your grasp of its predisposing conditions will influence a given outcome. This type of reasoning also goes by the name logical reasoning. Here is an example:

1.   First premise: If plants can make their food, then I must be a ghost

2.   Second premise: Photosynthesis allows plants to make their food

3.   Conclusion: I am a ghost

Now, the validity of the premise is inconsequential to the reasoning process that derives your conclusion. You may disagree with a given proposition, but the deduction process that led to the outcome is still correct, however inconceivable it may be. In the example given, you may not agree that plants make their food, but you cannot discount the conclusion that I am a ghost.

Your inference ends in a specific manner because the factors that influence it will support it to be that way. This reasoning method leads to conclusions that do not let you wander outside of the conditions presented to you. Your conclusions strictly follow the terms set by your previous premises.

Deductive reasoning is associated with logical thinkers, for example, mathematicians and data managers. It is common in skills, which require abundant logical thinking, such as calculations.

Inductive Reasoning

Inductive reasoning allows you to make conclusions based on previous experience. A series of repetitive occurrences influence your reasoning process to come up with your specific inference. Your determination depends on your perceived high level of probability or likelihood.

Here is an example:

1.   First premise: The stock prices have been trending upwards at the beginning of every third quarter since this company started

2.   Second premise: This year's third quarter starts next month

3.   Conclusion: This company's stock prices will go up next month

As you can see, we can conclude based on previous experience. This reasoning skill is crucial when predicting a future unknown based on past trends. As shown in the stock market example above, traders can make predictions on future stock movements based on already known past market trends. As long as the relevant past patterns maintain consistency, your predicted conclusions are, therefore, highly probable.

Abductive Reasoning

In this reasoning method, your conclusions will depend on the level of inter-relationship between available conditions. Here, you use your gut feeling to come up with your inference. You have a hunch that thing A has a relationship with thing B, and as a result, situation X has to be true. You come up with a probable conclusion by comparing observations that seem connected in your view. Your determination is therefore, based on a hunch or an educated guess.

Here is an example:

1.   First premise: Water freezes at tropical locations

2.   Second premise: Gasoline turns into vapor in arctic locations

3.   Conclusion: Water has a higher boiling point than gasoline (this becomes your hypothesis)

As you may notice, your conclusion may or may not be factually correct. However, to determine its factuality, your outcome will have to go through a validity test such as laboratory experimentation. You will find that nobody can fully agree or disagree with your inferences until he or she carries out a confirmation. It is common in scientific circles, especially when coming up with theories about a previously unknown subject. A scientific researcher will use the seeming similarities between his observations to propose a hypothesis. His hypothesis is then experimentally tested, and if found accurate, it becomes a theory through adoption.

Retroductive Reasoning

This reasoning method allows you to conclude based on already known factual conditions. You get to put forward a given inference to account for a series of known occurrences. For example, if A and B are present, then you expect to find C. In this case, the presence of C is conditional on A and B, and therefore, you have inverse reasoning. You almost seem to reason backward from a specific conclusion to confirm your suspicion of its contributing factors. This belief has its base on your previous experience and is slightly akin to inductive reasoning. However, the difference is that you do not have to predict an unknown future or heavily rely on probability. C is consequential as a result of A and B. Your conclusion serves almost like a confirmation of your hunch. You will use this reasoning trend as an experienced police detective when investigating crimes that you know follow a given pattern. You use clues and evidence to point you in a specific direction towards identifying suspects and their motives. Another application of this reasoning is in the health care system. Doctors will use your symptoms and signs to come up with a specific diagnosis. The health professionals know that certain patient symptoms are often indicative of a known malady. Since all human anatomy is similar, chances are the diagnosis will be correct.

In conclusion, sound reasoning is a great way to exercise your mind in the skill of abstract thinking. Getting your brain to draw intelligent conclusions based on a given set of premises is an ability consistent with good critical thinkers. Also, you can effectively defend or critically challenge a given position regarding a controversial subject based on proven sound reasoning skills.

Critical Thinking in Textual Analysis

From time to time, in our world of communication, you will encounter different types of text messages whose purpose is to convey specific information. You will come across news reports whose aim is to inform or fictional stories whose intention is to entertain. Myths and legends stimulate your imagination. Besides, you may encounter seemingly factual articles and opinion columns whose objectives are often subject to interpretation.

When gathering ideas or information from such written text, your final inference must match what the writer intended. However, if not, your understanding of the same article should have the capacity to query the validity of the implied conclusions. To achieve this ability, you will need to learn the skill of critical thinking in textual analysis. When applying this skill, you must always practice the following:

Read the material analytically

Critical reading involves understanding the content of the written information. You carefully and actively analyze the material as presented and try to see whether you know its premise. This reading method profoundly influences your comprehension of the specific message. However, you should be careful to read the text as it is and not as you would want it to be. Do not assume the intended meaning of the written message. This critical reading method would expose any ambiguity and passive text that would compromise your understanding. Therefore, to understand the written text truly, you need to apply your critical reading skills.

Think critically

Critical thinking is dependent on analytical reading. You can only draw conclusions based on what you have adequately understood. Your understanding is dependent on the clarity of the message; hence, the need for prior critical reading. Critical thinking involves challenging the assertions made by the text based on your opinions and understanding of the arguments presented.

Do you agree or disagree with the writer's inference? Critical thinking enables you to conclude, which may or may not differ from the writer's intended purpose. In addition to a difference in opinions, your other findings may also depend on current conventions or universally accepted facts.

Be objective

When analyzing text, objectivity demands that you set aside your assumptions and inherent beliefs. You will need to completely abandon your notions and assumptions and read the material as presented by the author. A common misstep by most readers is assuming the author's intentions and meanings based on their own experience.

This unacceptable practice is hugely subjective and results in a reader's bias. Your bias compromises objectivity as your critical reading is distorted.

As you know, this leads to poor analytical skills, which further affects your critical thinking down the line. Your ability to question the author's assertions independently becomes non-existent. To maintain an independent mind, you should always maintain objectivity.

Recognize the structure of the message

This skill allows you to see how the contents are being put together to achieve the author's intended objective. You can quickly surmise the flow of ideas within the author's stream of sentences and words used in the text. Another characteristic you would use to identify the structure is the use of examples by the author. You should find out if those examples are relevant to the point of the message.

You could conduct evidence-based scrutiny to determine the strengths of the author's illustrations. Do they distort the message or add to its relevance? How the paragraphs are arranged and spaced should allow you to move from one main idea to the next effortlessly. A good text analyzer would identify any shortcomings with the flow of ideas and the organization structure. Having this ability would enable you to offer criticism of the written material constructively and provide suitable alternatives to the author. Doing this will further boost your critical reading skills.

Draw your inference

Inferences are the conclusions you derive from the material. This overall take-home message is what you come up with at the end of the whole text material. Therefore, as opposed to critical reading, this stage will involve critical thinking on your part. As mentioned earlier, your critical thinking skills come in handy when making assertions and inferences during this stage. You should try to visualize and have an overall mental picture of your understanding of the content. In addition to this big-picture view, you should tap into your emotions to find out how it made you feel.

Has the article left you emotionally changed from how you felt before reading it? What was the overall tone and mood of the article? Combining these two inputs, i.e., big mental picture and emotional implications, should allow you to make your inference independent of outside influence.

Describe the material in your own words. Your ability to come up with a separate take-home message highly depends on your base knowledge. This fundamental skill is your application of objective and critical reading that is void of bias and assumptions.

Raise queries and challenges

First, identify the writer's conclusions. Once you come up with your inference, compare it to the author's findings. Do they match? Do you disagree with the author's conclusions? Your critical thinking skills, which have guided you this far, will allow you to argue for or against any conclusions. You can provide alternative counterclaims to those of the author. You may also have a different point of view using other stronger arguments.

Your ability to come up with valuable questions at the end of your reading is essential if you are to provide constructive criticism. The ability to offer criticism or counterclaims depends on your ability to formulate viable arguments that challenge the author's assertions and assumptions. During such challenges, you may imagine yourself as having a one on one debate with the author arguing for or against the inferred position.

Book critics often have an uncanny ability to offer counterarguments even in the most unlikely scenarios. If you are considering such a career, then you should always possess a curious mind. Remember, you cannot challenge that which you do not understand, and you must always have an alternative if you disagree with a given inference.

How You Apply Sound Reasoning and Textual Analysis

Critical thinking in sound reasoning is a deliberate process that exercises your analytical mind. This activity is a process that improves your reasoning skills over time and expands your intrinsic knowledge. Critical thinking challenges your automatically accepted norms and assumptions. Your default beliefs and viewpoints may not necessarily be the universal truths you thought they were. In everyday life, your ability to decipher implied meanings, metaphors, analogies, or abstract concepts boosts your mental capacity. Besides, your sound knowledge improves through the continued application of deductive reasoning skills. Critical thinking allows you to defend your viewpoints using appropriate evidence or open your mind to previously unseen perspectives.

Critical thinking in the textual analysis is a useful skill when writing articles and opinion pieces based on factual references. You will want the reader to comprehensively understand your flow of ideas and eventually come to the same conclusion as you intended. On the other hand, book critics use this skill when reviewing article submissions and offering constructive criticisms. In higher education, you may use these skills in writing and effectively defending your specific thesis. This ability allows you to validate your viewpoints through challenging queries and counterarguments.

To apply your critical thinking skills in your daily life effectively, consider doing the following:

Verify claims before concluding

This habit is vital, especially in this climate of fake news. You should always question the validity of seeming truths by verifying their validity. Always exercise caution before accepting any information being spewed by the media as absolute truth. You are encouraged to use multiple sources to verify the validity of any news article.

Interested parties that want to influence your opinions to their nefarious often use fake news for their benefit. Such parties will target your trust in the honesty of the media. Always rely on trusted media houses or known authentic news sources. Learn to question opinions and do not be hasty to accept ideas at face value. Remember to ask yourself whether an article is too good to be true, and if so, then it probably is.

Entertain differing opinions

Do not be rigid in your preconceptions. Be open to other various opinions. You should learn to consider the viewpoints that are different from your own seriously. Try to understand why others view a specific subject the way that they do. This simple action will open up your mind to the various possible angles of looking at a particular issue. Besides, your intrinsic knowledge on a subject expands beyond your previously rigid perspective. You broaden your horizon, and in certain situations, you may have a change in attitude.

However, if you still do not agree with a differing opinion, entertain it. This action will let you understand why others reason the way they do. As a result, you learn to live and coexist with tolerance. You may also find those specific aspects of their viewpoints align with your own. A little tinkering or tweaking such aspects converts what seemed like vast differences between people into a minor misunderstanding.

Evaluate the implications of your held perspective

You may expose the shortcomings of a held belief by challenging its potential consequences. Always try to consider the implications of your held viewpoint. Rather than questioning a specific perspective, you could examine all its effects. For instance, views on subjective matters usually have contradicting implications. Such issues deal with differences in climate change, religion, and science.

Resolve your differences with logic and evidence

Whenever you run into a difference in opinions, it is vital to strengthen your argument position using evidence and logical reasoning. Applying sound reasoning skills in cases of conflicting opinions will go a long way to prove your point or weaken the opposing side position. Using everyday examples as evidence for your situation would make it easily relatable to the other's stand.

Most of your differences are usually minor misunderstandings in specific aspects and not the whole premise. You should bolster your points using calm and deliberate explanations with abundant evidence in real life.

For instance, you can argue your position of rotating earth around a static sun against a mobile sun transiting across the sky. You may evidence the sun always rising from the east and setting in the west at regular time intervals. Also, using inductive reasoning based on weather and climate patterns, you can predict weather forecasts to disprove an opposing belief in rain gods. This resolution technique applies both ways also, i.e., if the evidence does not support your argument, then it is wise to reconsider your position.

Be open to change

You may be wrong in your long-held beliefs and assumptions. In such cases, you should be open to re-evaluating your perspective when presented with evidence to the contrary. To err is human and so you should be free to alter your viewpoint. This flexibility to change is useful whenever the evidence contradicts your views, or a confirmatory experiment disproves your hypothesis. It is advisable not to rely on many educated guesses. You may want to eliminate any of your beliefs that exist on a hunch.

As mentioned earlier, critical thinking is the skillful conceptualizing analysis and evaluation of information to form a judgment or conclusion. Critical thinking allows you to be open to receiving ideas and arguments. It examines logic and reasoning to form a judgment. Critical thinkers try to understand the information given by asking questions and examining the answers using logic and reasoning without jumping into conclusions. They do not just receive information and accept them, but they always search for the truth in the message given.

For critical thinking to be successful, we need to have certain skills such as listening, analysis, evaluation, and interpretation.

Chapter 2:
Mind Mapping

A mind map is a diagram used to organize information visually. A brain map is hierarchical and reveals relationships among portions of the entire world. It's frequently created around one idea, drawn as a picture in the middle of a blank page, so that related representations of thoughts such as pictures, words and parts of phrases are included. Important ideas are linked directly to the fundamental idea, along with other thoughts branching out from these significant ideas.

Mind maps are also drawn by hand, equally as "notes" during a lecture, meeting or planning session, as an instance, or as high-quality images when more time can be obtained. Mind maps are regarded as a kind of spider structure.

Much like additional diagramming tools, mind maps may be utilized to create, visualize, construction, and categorize ideas, as well as an aid to analyze and organize data, solve problems, make conclusions, and compose.

Besides those direct usage cases, data recovered from brain maps may be utilized to boost a lot of different programs, such as expert search programs, search engines and research and label query recommender. To accomplish this, mind maps could be analyzed with classic procedures of data retrieval to categorize a brain map's writer or files that are linked from inside the brain map.

A mind map is a simple way to brainstorm thoughts without fretting about arrangement and construction. It permits you to structure your thoughts visually to assist with analysis and remember.

A mind map is a diagram for representing jobs, words, theories, or things linked to a fundamental idea or topic with a non-linear graphical design, which makes it possible for the user to construct an intuitive frame around a fundamental idea. A mind map may flip a long collection of dull information into a vibrant, memorable, and highly organized diagram that operates in accord with your mind's natural method of doing things.

A mind map may be utilized as a simplified content management system (CMS). It lets you keep all of your information in a centralized place to remain organized. With the variety of mind mapping computer software programs available now, you can attach documents to various branches for even more versatility. You can also switch to different various perspectives to find one that is best for you. Mind mapping stimulates and challenges you and your staff for brainstorming actions. You will detect some amazing facts about your mind and its purpose and simply take the first significant step on the road to liberty of the brain.

n extremely effective method for getting advice, thoughts, and theories in and outside of your mind -- it is a creative and plausible way of Jelqing and note-making that literally 'maps outside' your thoughts.

All mind maps have a few things in common. They've a natural organizational structure that radiates in the middle and uses symbols, lines, color and graphics based on easy, brain-friendly theories. A brain map converts a long collection of dull information into a vibrant, memorable, and extremely organized diagram that operates in accord with your mind's natural way of doing things.

One simple way to comprehend mind mapping would be to compare it to a map of a town. The town center represents the most important idea; the key streets leading in the center represent the essential ideas on your thinking process; the secondary streets or branches signify your secondary ideas, and so forth. Particular shapes or images may represent landmarks of curiosity or especially relevant thoughts.

The brain map is the outside mirror of your radiant or natural believing facilitated by a highly effective graphic procedure that offers the universal key to unlock the energetic potential of their mind.

Mind view enables you to think and learn visually by creating mind maps. It's been shown to boost organizational abilities and imagination to create memory retention and deepen comprehension of theories. Not only can it be demonstrated that brain mapping raises learning, memory and thinking abilities, but also the usage of multimedia presentations (incorporating images, videos, sounds etc.) and strongly enhances comprehension and retention of data. Head view is optimized for brain mapping, planning and storyboarding websites, and multimedia presentations.

A mind map is a graphic way to represent ideas and theories. It's a visual thinking tool that helps structure info, assisting you to analyze, understand, synthesize, remember, and create new ideas. As in every excellent concept, its power lies in its simplicity.

In a mind map, instead of a conventional note or linear text, data is organized in a manner that looks more carefully at how your mind really works. As it's an activity that's both artistic and analytical, it engages your mind in a much richer manner, assisting in all of its cognitive capabilities. And, on top of that, it's fun!

Mind mapping is a kind of visual thinking done by composing one's thoughts in the kind of images or other graphic representation, such as spider diagrams, to get as clear a picture of this topic in question as you can.

It's an employed technique that bridges notions and thoughts. You start by writing down the center idea or thought in the midst of a bit of paper then branch out in all directions together with applicable info and ideas that relate to and create in the first core idea. These associated ideas can then become the cornerstone of additional ideas, and these additional ideas will continue the procedure into fourth grade thoughts and so forth etc.

Possessing a listing on an entire page and then more pages of lists could be a bit daunting and result in confusion; therefore, mind mapping with colors, with an emphasis on words, for example, use of symbols and patterns to help explain thoughts and make inspiration and focus - all of that boosts motivation.

What do you use mind mapping for?

You can use mind mapping for virtually anything, and it'll enable your motivation in many things. Psychologists, teachers, engineers and other careers that require intensive believing prior to coming to a finish, use mind mapping. It's frequently utilized in business and trade and workplace surroundings. It may be located in training such as brainstorming that are mind maps drawn immediately with flip charts and whiteboards and other websites. It's the thoughts instead of the mind map that are significant in brainstorming. Participation of trainees and workers all add to increase ideas concerning how the true thoughts map may be developed. This exercise can help to reinforce concepts and thoughts more than the usual record ever could!

Additionally, it helps to organize individuals and store info to be able to find out things by remembering the procedure for producing the map particularly. In junior or primary college, mind mapping is introduced into interactive classes that are a lot more stimulating, engaging, and inspiring and contribute to kids displaying more excitement in sorting, organizing and motivation towards keeping information. Mind mapping can raise kids' purpose and learning capability, and this is especially useful once the child or young person is revising or taking notes in class or in lectures. It's the procedure of creating a mind site in which the learning happens, not the final result.

This is only because you're using one-word thoughts or phrases, visual thinking or logos or graphics and graphic representations that have deeper significance for you as well as fit in with the larger image or concept. This helps immensely with memory and remembering that's much more uplifting and inspiring and can lessen the shortage of motivation many frequently experience or connect with revision normally.

Mind mapping is excellent for self-motivation too, so utilize it in your personal life. It can allow you to create and attain significant decisions more quickly and readily.

Going over your head mapping points later, then you might have the ability to determine adverse or unfavorable traits for deeper thought. Therefore, additional subbranches may include the following theories:

Passionate - constantly occupied with many things, also assertive, rigid, likely to be argumentative.

Has a great job - workaholic, suffers from anxiety, brings home issues from work, no work/life equilibrium.

When you make a mind map and brainstorm matters, writing the first things that come into your mind then looking at it can sometimes describe things straight off by viewing the benefits and pitfalls of any situation immediately. This frequently motivates you to make a decision there and then.

Mind maps cut much of this evaluation that you get from performing lists. Too much research contributes to paralysis, and it is the most frequent illness that slows down advances in several facets of our lives. It may conquer decision making so much with an effect for many that the choice is no more applicable from the time that it's made.

In essence, you're using your intuition and subconscious procedure when doing mind mapping. You're using your five senses to process and report information, not only info in the surroundings, but also information accessible internally from previous knowledge and experiences, which lets you make better choices.

In general, it's a fantastic instrument. Life's problems would not be called "hurdles" if there was not a means to get them over. Accessing and using the power of instinct through mind mapping comes in an awareness of what is occurring in the entire body (felt feeling) in addition to the brain, and this aspect is essential for using your instinct for making better choices, making your revision simpler and more engaging. All this contributes to getting over the barriers, much more motivation, better consciousness and getting things done.

So why is mind mapping deemed to be such a potent instrument. To know why, it's very important to comprehend the idea behind these diagrams. In the event that you should see a brain cell, you'd observe a hexagon such as nucleus with a spindle like branches coming out of it and linking to other cells. Brain cells communicate with each other through those nerve pathways that seem like branches.

So, when you're mind mapping, you're mirroring how the brain maps out and communicates its own thought processes. However, there's another significant role and purpose to brain mapping, which is that, if you participate in this procedure, it pushes the ideal side of their mind to talk and speak with the remaining side of their mind.

When you employ this technique, you are plugging a difference that many have, and that's the absence of balance between left and right brain thinking. Most are left brain dominant in how they process information.

The left has to do with the rational and logical processes involved in believing. The right brain consists of the innovative and ingenious thought processes that involve procedures like visualization, rhythm, and instinct like music.

Logic alone informs us that we've been extended a left and right side to the mind with distinct but equally significant contributions to make to the practice of believing, yet the majority of us don't utilize our entire brain.

Mind mapping is one method of assisting to restore this balance, since it promotes lateral thinking where left and right brain need to communicate with each other longer. I find that, if folks try to mind map, at first, it seems somewhat like 'palms and thumbs' since they're forming new patterns of communicating ideas whilst undoing learned customs.

After you write text onto a webpage at the traditional educated form from left to right, that's a linear type of thinking on paper; that isn't how the mind thinks. Studies have demonstrated that people only remember 20 percent of what we read by text independently.

After just a little practice with thought maps, individuals begin to enjoy this process and realize the worth of doing this. It's possible to head map on paper, or it is also possible to use a mind mapping program. Using paper to begin with assists to develop the ability.

However, using applications makes it considerably more potential than direct usage of paper. As an instance, mind-mapping software permits you to attach files in one map, so you've got them in one area to refer to, rather than having to maintain opening files that are different. Additionally, it lets you web conference and determine different gifts and upgrades to a specific job being worked on, replacing the need to sail to meeting areas to satisfy the identical purpose.

When implemented properly, mind mapping streamlines the process of company growth and personal advancement, thus saving time in addition to increasing productivity, creativity, and learning functionality.

Part of the achievement of mind mapping as learning and thinking tool is that its use of color and graphics excite the brain whilst the arrangement of branches mirrors how the brain stores its own memories. It's this that can help us operate through a procedure to embed new words to our memory and will produce an extremely beneficial crib sheet to fall back on.

There are additional methods of utilizing linguistic institutions and eccentric wordplay and visualization to incorporate language, and they have their place, yet this procedure employs the mind map arrangement to classify and organize words.

Additionally, you now have a picture mind map to check your recall of this language and image/word variant to test yourself against and work as a point of reference before you do not want it and have become eloquent in that language.

In addition, the most important thing is that the entire thing could have been interesting, a lot more engaging, and no doubt a great deal of fun.

What thoughts mapping does is choose these brainstorming ideas as they develop and set them in a pattern that is focused on that subject or issue. So, imagine, when you develop with every thought, every truth, each and every bit of information and then you use a brain map, each and everything is allocated to a department or section of the map. This gives precious relationships and interconnectedness, which you will not have considered.

You physically watch, or can decide, how one idea relates to the other. In brainstorming, a lot of the relationships are not clear or don't reveal the chances they can generate. Head maps supply the cross-fertilization, the evolution of new thoughts, so beneficial in the imaginative process and for greater productivity. They are especially valuable for entrepreneurs when confronted with having to employ a winning business proposition. For students, there is no better method of making up a workable subject for their own essay or term paper.

This is a brain map about -- handily enough -- head mapping itself. Its gifts, in a visual manner, the core components, and techniques about the best way best to draw thoughts maps.

Benefits and programs

Fundamentally, mind mapping stops dull and linear thinking. It runs your imagination and ensure pleasure.

However, what do we use mind maps for?

- Note carrying
- Brainstorming (independently or in groups)
- Problem solving
- Assessing and memorization
- Planning
- Assessing and consolidating information from multiple resources
- Presenting information
- Gaining insight on complicated subjects
- Running your imagination

It is difficult to do justice to the amount of applications mind maps may have -- the reality is they can help explain your thinking about virtually anything in several distinct contexts: personal, household, educational or company. Planning one day or planning your own life, outlining a book, starting a job, creating and planning presentations, composing blog articles -well, you get the idea -- anything, actually.

o brings a mind map

Drawing a mind map is as straightforward as 1-2-3:

- Start at the middle of a blank webpage, drawing or writing the thought you wish to develop. I'd recommend that you utilize the page in landscape orientation.

- Build the associated subtopics around this fundamental topic, linking each of them into the center with a lineup.

- Duplicate the exact same procedure for those subtopics, creating lower-level subtopics as you see fit, linking all these into the corresponding subtopic.

Some more recommendations:

- Utilize colors, symbols and drawings copiously. Be visual as possible, and your mind will thank you. I have met many men and women who do not even attempt this with the excuse they are "not artistic." Do not let this keep you from trying it out.

- Maintain the subject labels as brief as possible, keeping them into one word -- or, even better, to merely a picture. Notably on mind maps, the urge to compose a comprehensive term is tremendous, but constantly search for opportunities to shorten it into one word or figure -- your own thoughts map will probably be more successful that way.

- Vary text size, color, and orientation. Vary the depth and duration of these lines. Supply as many visual cues as possible to highlight important points. Every little bit helps engage your mind.

Chapter 3:
Analysis Techniques

Brainstorming

The brainstorming is where a bunch of people get together and they start bringing ideas to the table with the hope of finding solutions to whatever their problem is, it is an effective way that solves many big problems.

So, let us focus on how brainstorming techniques can help you to generate new ideas and to find innovative solutions to difficult problems.

Brainstorming meetings:

When Brainstorming meetings are done well, they open up possibilities and break down assumptions because everyone participates in the building of ideas. It promotes buy-in. Buy-in in this case refers to getting agreement to support a decision because not only brainstorming meetings can often be fun, but they can also have the added benefit of bonding a group of individuals together. But unfortunately, this benefit can be undermined by criticism that is offered too early or one powerful voice that unfortunately quiets others. The best ideas come from brainstorming meetings where everyone feels safe to throw ideas into the mix.

Effective Brainstorming Session:

Some people think a brainstorming session is just about free-for-all outside of the box crazy idea generation and it is, but it will be more effective if you set some parameters. Let us have a look at them.

• Firstly, you define the problem and the brainstorm is supposed to solve that problem.

• Then you set criteria that the idea needs to meet. For example, the boss clearly identified that the goal was to brainstorm; what makes herbal toothpaste and breath mints stand out products in the market and then you need to brainstorm as many names as possible.

• You also need to consider who should attend the smaller groups because smaller groups tend to work better than large groups; if you do have a large group consider creating smaller breakout groups. However, when creating your group take people of different backgrounds and experiences because they offer a wider variety of ideas.

• You also need to think about how much time to devote to the brainstorming session because it is not called brainstorming for nothing; the mental work required of brainstorming means such meetings are best kept short. If a rigorous brainstorming session is revved for too long, your head feels like it is on fire. It is great but it is exhausting as well. It can be a challenge to know when to close but a good rule of thumb is if you are generating ideas keep it to 30 to 40 minutes long. If the session begins to lag or slow down, just wrap it up. On the other hand, if you are making connections and creating frameworks and the creative sparks are flying then make it longer because there is nothing worse than breaking the concentration in the middle of the creative process.

The Hybrid model:

When it comes to the brainstorming session what method you should prefer? Should you do it as a group and discuss ideas as they come up? Should you start brainstorming alone and then come together with others who have also brainstorm alone to share and discuss your ideas? So, which method do you think is more effective? And when brainstorming for innovation would you rather have an outcome of one outstanding idea along with several pretty bad ideas or would you rather have many average and good ideas?

The average quality in the hybrid model was 30% higher than the average in the traditional group model and the quality for the top five ideas in each group as well as and the quality of the best idea were both higher in the hybrid model. They found that initial independent thoughts were unbiased and unaffected by external circumstances; so, in other words people were less likely to censor themselves to go along with a superior or to leave a heavy lifting or hard work to others.

You can implement the hybrid model in one of two ways; first, you can have people brainstorm independently before the meeting and offer some guidance to ensure enough ideas have been generated. For example, you can tell them come up with at least 10 ideas by Wednesday.

Another option is to give time in the brainstorm meeting for everyone to silently write down ideas before discussing them as a group.

Rules for Brainstorming:

Regardless of the method, you choose you should follow certain guidelines for the brainstorming session to ensure success.

• First, establish the ground rules; for example, discourage criticism of ideas because the purpose of brainstorming is idea generation and evaluating the merits of the ideas can come later.

• You should encourage building on other ideas because this is not about ownership of an idea. And at the same time, you do not want to focus too much on only building one idea.

• Then enlist the help of a scribe to capture all the ideas in a visible location. You can use a flip chart a whiteboard or even better an online brainstorming tool, even something as simple as Google Docs because that allows everyone to contribute at once whether they are in the room or across the globe. This can sometimes also allow a means for anonymous brainstorming which can help encourage participation use mind maps to show connections between your ideas, but whatever you do keep the mood positive and the energy level high.

• Then break the process up into several shorter meetings if start to lag.

• So, in short you can generate the highest quality ideas, incorporate a hybrid model of individual and then group brainstorming, bring together a diverse group of people so that you have many different perspectives; define the problem or set the criteria; document the ideas and postpone evaluation and keep the energy level high.

Mind Storming

Mind storming is about understanding the answer to all your questions that are inside you. It answers to all of your questions that are inside you; you just need to tap into the infinite knowledge and get what you need because infinite knowledge is the universal intelligence coming from the source of it. You all must have ever had the experience where you ask a question quietly to yourself in your mind and then out of nowhere you get the answer from inside of you and that is such an amazing experience. It happens quite a lot especially when you are quiet or in meditation or just quietly listening to yourself that is why you have to learn to ask questions all of the time and ask them to yourself and then listen yourself.

It is important to look up the questions themselves and search for more but it is more important to learn to listen to yourself and that is what you will learn in meditation; you ask and then then listen.

Therefore, there is this technique that you can learn to do the mind storming. You need to get a blank piece of paper and you write your goal at the top. In the meanwhile, no negative thoughts are allowed when you are writing it down so that you do not end up sabotaging yourself and it leads you backwards. Then the next thing you need is energy; energy is important in this too so you must get into the action like how the law of attraction says; you attract to yourself what you are but you must also get into the action and do your part. So, put this technique into action and be an achiever in life.

The Pareto Principle

What is the Pareto principle? The Pareto principle is an expression of a very general principle in nature.

The Pareto principle is the most helpful concept of time, of life and of management.

So, how is this valuable for you? Well, first find a vital few problem and resolve them then find the vital few sources of risk and mitigate those and then find your vital few stakeholders and satisfy them. The Pareto principle, the 80/20 rule, and the law of the vital few tells us that if we prioritize ruthlessly, we can find a small number of points of control and use those points of control to gain significant leverage over anything

80/20 Rule in life

We can take Pareto's 80/20 rule and apply it to almost any situation but in particular we can apply it to goal setting and productivity in life. Because according to this principle 20% of your activities will account for 80% of your results that means if you have a list of 10 items to accomplish then two of those items will turn out to be worth more than the other 8 other items put together. However, the sad fact is that most people procrastinate on the top 10 or 20 percent of items that are the most valuable and important.

Step 1: What is your most important goal in life right now and you need to know this most important goal if you want to be successful. Then pick the second most important goal for yourself. Then what you will find is that after you complete this exercise you will have determined the most important 20% of your goals that will help you more than anything else you do.

Step 2: Then you should work at those goals that you have chosen all the time. They can actually change your whole future.

The rule for this is simple; resist the temptation to clear up small things first because that is the greatest killer. We become so involved in little things and that little things multiply they just become more and more at the end of the day and become your disaster and you have not accomplished anything. If you choose to start your day working on low value tasks then you will soon develop the habit of always starting and working on low tasks and you will be like a horse that pulls the wheel around in a circle all day never makes any progress.

A study has just been done about the attitudes of rich people versus poor people. What they found is that 85% of rich people have one big goal that they work on all the time only 3% of poor people have a big goal and they do not work on it very much. Therefore, if you want to be wealthy then do what wealthy people do; pick one big goal and work on it all the time and if you do it then it will change your life. When your goals are clear then you will come up with the right answer to achieve your goals at the right time.

So, in this way you can apply the 80/20 rule to goal setting in your life then you can achieve anything you desire. If you want to change your future, take action.

While the Pareto principle has seen a few decades pass into the inception but the theory behind the principle is timeless. It is even in writing as 80% of writing in speech is 20% of words and similarly, people wear 20% of their clothes 80% of the time. It is even been boiled down to a formula for use in mathematics.

Examples:

Have you ever noticed that 80% of a business's sales come from just 20% of customers? So that 80% of the work is done by 20% of people. Or maybe that 80% of customer service issues arise from 20% of customers. It turns out that there is a well-documented phenomenon that occurs not just in business but also in nature. It often turns out to be the case that 80% of a business's sales volume is generated by 20% of its customer base. In other words, most businesses have dedicated base of super fans.

Some business examples of the Pareto principle are that 80% of your profits come from 20% of your key customers. 80% of your sales come from 20% of your key products or services. 80% of your successful campaigns will come from only 20% of your advertising. 20% of your sales force will produce 80 percent of your sales, etc. But the big question is do businesspeople really focus on the 20% customers? Well as can see that not all of the customers are created equal and 20% customers generate almost 80 percent of your revenue.

How to use 80/20 rule in business?

So, let us call the 20 percent as your ideal customers and consider the 80/20 rule in your customer ratio to understand how this can help your business. Almost all businesspeople know who their customers are but very few pay attention to who their ideal customer is; in every business their ideal customers are the backbone of business and it is easy to find out who your ideal customer is. Your ideal customer is someone who is very happy with your products and services; he or she not only religiously and repeatedly use your products but also bring in more customers to you. Ideal customers are excited about your new offerings and they are the ones who will grab your products the very moment they are launched; they are your raving fans. Every successful business has ideal customers or raving fans they keep coming back to you for more. If you look into your total business revenue you can find that the 20% group known as the key accounts. It is not that the customers you lack in business but what you lack is the number of ideal customers who belong to the 20% group that is responsible for your 80% profits.

Imagine you can increase your ideal customers to a hundred percent then your business will grow almost four times. Many customers who are in the bracket of 80 percent can be converted into your ideal customer base or you could extend your marketing to reach out to more new ideal customers if you are selling products and services. Identify the

20% of your customer base that is bringing in 80 percent of your profits and strengthen your relationships with them; enhance the products and services they are investing. You must try to make sense of your ideal customers and find out the commonality that binds the ideal customer base and reach out to more ideal customers and you will see your business grow. Similarly, if you can use this rule it will help you to have clarity on other areas like managing people or team customer service, sales, business development, etc.

You have the opportunity to turn many customers into 20 percenters whether that is through oil tea programs or customer advocacy moments of delight for VIPs. Therefore, this is how you can give something back to your most loyal customers and in turn get them excited about returning to your business in spending more money.

Chapter 4:
Benefits of Critical Thinking

How often do you hear the question, "Come Down To Earth, and think critically?" It is likely common to hear from family, students, teachers, and other people who have already seen the world and can agree that the practice of consciously learning about a subject or concept without having feelings or opinions to influence you is the best way to deal with this environment. But is it valid at all times?

The essay attempts to provide you with both the benefits of critical thinking and its drawbacks with a rational answer to these questions. Make confident that in everyday life you can discover the golden mean of using critical thinking skills.

One Side of the coin: 5 advantages of Critical Thinking

- The ability to think logically and rationally.
- The ability to interpret facts objectively.
- The ability to understand the logical connection between ideas.
- The ability to make informed decisions, etc.

Let's find out why it is considered useful for these abilities.

1. You Are Able to evaluate issues without Bias

Most people approach things differently—one depends on their values, perceptions, feelings, or the thoughts of somebody else. All this influences how you deal with one issue or another, especially with such controversial topics as abortion, death penalty, animal testing, or immigration. With solid evidence, there are many questions to be answered. Moreover, what's going to help you get it? Yes, critical thinking lets you collect and analyze relevant information and accurately translate it for sound conclusions and solutions.

2. You can foresee how things will turn out

Willpower, intelligence, expertise, inspiration, understanding of the right people, being in the right place, and time is all that makes a person successful in the modern world. And yet, there's another aspect that allows progress to be accomplished—it's the ability to predict what's going to happen and need in the future. How can it be? Analytically and critically, you know the current issues by recognizing the logical connections between ideas and arguments. For example, Heather A. Butler researched 244 participants with her collaborators, Christopher Pentoney, Mabelle P. Bong, to investigate the importance of critical thinking and intellectual to forecasting real-world outcomes. Consequently, it is known that critical thinking is a better predictor of real-world outcomes than knowledge. So, start developing your critical thinking skills right now to know what's going to happen in various important areas–economics, industry, advertising, sales, etc.

3. You Communicate with Others Sharing Your Ideas Effectively

It is crucial to get a message out to the target audience–be it your boss, peers, or professors–when you analyze a question and forecast the possible outcomes. Critical thinking usually detaches all our thoughts from the public expression of an argument. Only have a realistic view of the situation at hand and how to solve a problem by collaborating with friends or other individuals together. Simultaneously, open mind for a different view that you can also perceive with the help of recognizing valid logic.

4. You are trusted to figure out solutions to complex problems

It is particularly valuable when a person can define, evaluate problems and even systematically predict and solve them rather than by intuition or instinct. In this case, it means that you are guaranteed career promotion. It will also have an overall impact on your life. Indeed, addressing complex issues is a great responsibility. But imagine how many difficult questions you might be able to answer if you put your critical thinking skills into practice.

5. You are highly appreciated by employers

If critical thinking is one of your attributes, you have already been demonstrated the opportunities in a professional career. What do students usually do when they graduate from college or university? "Where can I find my dream job? "For students, this is a common question. That's why in critical thinking if you want to excel immediately in a job search, continue to succeed. Many firms search for critical thinkers, communicative, constructive, and innovative career candidates.

The Flip Side to the Coin: 5 disadvantages of Critical Thinking

Critical thinking is considered as important as breathing in some situations. Like in an interview, or perhaps when you do a test, but not always. In childhood, when you were asked, "What would you like to be? " And you might automatically answer,' I want to be a journalist when I grow up,' or' I dream of becoming an artist,' but then you grew up, and all the innocence and positive outlook were destroyed when life's realities and practicalities crashed against you.

Critical thinking is the dream-killer. One minute you'll dream of being the greatest artist of all times, and you'll notice the huge, gaping holes in your plan when you start to analyze it critically. You're going to start having second thoughts and facing endless dilemmas. Are you going to have to move to another city? Have you the ability to become an artist? Are you competitive? The list continues and continues.

You may be proud of your ability to think critically at any stage, but here are some examples that can be detrimental to you.

1. All of a sudden, your peer's jokes make no sense to you, and they are no longer funny. How many times have you rolled your eyes at them because you automatically think "amateur hour" when you hear one of their repeated jokes! And you're just frowning when they want you to smile.

2. You care too much about gender equality

If your girlfriend/boyfriend gushes over that amazing invitation you received to a party to come, and you forget about gender equality. Don't you think you have a little different idea?

3. You Feel Shame When Your Group Mates Speak

And when, as you would have thought, they are unable to express their thoughts in a reasonable, so intelligent manner, you feel sorry for your group mates and simultaneously feel ashamed that you talk about them this way and that you are like that.

4. You're alone with your books

Not only do you love novels, your mates will hate, but you can't talk to them about the finer points in the story because they'll probably think you've gone crazy. And they're smiling at you.

5. You Only Adequate Companion Is You

It's hard to admit, but you can only talk to yourself about really interesting issues. Who can think about climate change's bio cultural approach? Who knows why promoting solar energy is important?

Who is defending Severus Snape for doing everything he can to protect Harry? Sure, you are alone.

Okay, overall, critical thinking has its benefits and is quite useful in some situations (think about Sherlock Holmes, people!). But most of the time, it will leach out all the fun and exasperate the mates around you.

Businesses that want to remain competitive and profitable need to recruit critically thinking workers. Hiring a college graduate is not enough. New hires must be knowledgeable, logical, and strong problem-solvers. Strategic and critical thinking is the most needed skill by employers worldwide when evaluating job candidates, according to business surveys. The U.S. Labor Department has listed critical thinking, problem solving, decision-making, organizational strategy, and risk management as essential workplace skills. Employers demand that recruits have more than textbook knowledge and technical skills and agree that critical thinking is vital for job performance and career mobility. It was also revealed that critical thinking was considered the most important attribute to help their businesses grow, more than creativity or increased information technology.

Job conditions are increasingly pushing workers into new jobs. Employees can no longer rely on others to make key decisions and are forced to make them alone and quickly. Good decisions include concentrating on the most relevant information, asking the right questions, and believing correctly that too few workers possess these skills. A survey of Human Resource professionals (SHRM) found a total 70 percent of high school workers are deficient in critical thinking skills. In other recent studies, 45 percent of college graduates made no noticeable improvement in developing critical thinking or reasoning skills during college's first two years. After four years, 36% made no major gains in critical thinking skills. When these students leave school and enter the workforce, they will be unprepared for working world challenges. When managers say critical thinking skills are highly valued, applicants possessing these qualities will be in demand and difficult to find. Critical skills will become invaluable. The types of jobs and work environments evolve, versatility and adaptability will become essential to meeting real-world conditions and something that practitioners and recruiters need to test for in interviews. Developing critical thinking sets of your existing employees will also become important.

One strategy for management managers is to use pre-hiring planning tests. Individuals who score well on these assessments demonstrate good analytical skills, reasoning, decision-making, and efficiency. They often demonstrate the ability to evaluate the information value presented, are innovative, have better job knowledge, and often move up in your business. There are some tests of managerial and skilled applicants assessing hard skills. Research also shows that higher-level management roles require critical thinking skills and the ability to learn quickly and accurately process information. Organizations that include both critical thinking and personality tests in hiring practices will have a greater overall candidate perspective than organizations that use personality or critical thinking assessments alone.

Helping employees become strategic thinkers can be done by introducing questioning techniques. Better questioning helps to visualize better and synthesize information. By practice, this process can become automatic, with the ultimate goal of transferring information to new situations and scenarios. Some courses teach students to be good listeners, not great thinkers. Passive training does not inherently improve mental or behavioral skills. Active participation in the learning process will be more successful, providing more long-term results.

Knowledge acquired and interpreted by higher-order thought is recalled more than conventional memorization. Knowledge is easier to transfer and implement, leading to better problem solving. Questioning becomes a vital part of teaching and learning. Perfecting the questioning art begins with establishing what is known, allowing the instructor or mentor to develop new ideas and understandings. Questioning strategies can be used to promote students ' mentality. Create appropriate questions. Perform the strategy. Encourage open dialogue and participation.

Generally, open-ended questions lead students to explore and assess more effectively. A professional questioner's most important elements are asking short and concise questions, rephrasing, and extracting more responses from the student's answers. The practice must also master every ability. Offer your audience the opportunity to practice the ideas, skills, behaviors, and behavioral changes resulting from your questions and choose specific activities to enable them to reflect. Think of scenarios to bring your new employee or mentee to a scenario that builds on what they already know. It can be as easy as reading a rule, providing a real-life example of a situation, pointing something on a table or in person. Instead, design a problem showing the right thought process.

Propose a problem that can be solved collaboratively or through the scenario. Also, use an exploratory interrogation method. What if it were? Explain what just happened. What strategies worked or didn't work? What'd you do next time? What can we suppose? Maybe there's a discussion. What will happen next? Ultimately, provide some feedback or create opportunities for self-assessment. Use this advice to draw on your next lesson and never lose creative thinking. Learners won't want to replicate their actions unless they feel valued.

You'll know that when the problem is visualized, higher-order thought can be represented and clarified. The learner will also be able to distinguish between relevant and non-relevant data and will look for reasons why or why something is happening. You will rationalize and clarify why a solution works and see different angles or sides of a problem. Recall capitalizing on real-world situations.

This not only helps students use the data in the right reference frame but also helps you solve real-world problems in your company or business. Encourage your learner to think about the methods you're implementing, as this will demonstrate that this is a valuable method to adopt while solving problems over and over. If recruiters and managers start looking for employees with these skills and use the art of questioning for existing employees, critical thinking becomes invaluable for the future success of your organization. Companies hiring and developing critical thinkers have a competitive advantage. With these skills being hired, too few employees have opportunities to develop them in the workplace.

Evaluating Patterns of Thinking

Wisdom is adapting knowledge and experience to a given situation to make sound decisions. It's how we relate our awareness (how we know) and experience (what we've been through) to what we do (acting), what we feel (perception) and how we measure (judging). Wisdom means adding what we've heard. It's studying part-time. Therefore, wisdom comes from (an application). Without doing what we've heard, we can't get understanding. You can't read wisdom; you can't memorize wisdom; you can't repeat wisdom; you can't learn wisdom; you can only gain wisdom by practicing what you've written, memorized, studied and recited. Only by doing can one gain knowledge. Knowledge cannot be gained by silence (idleness); knowledge must be used (applied) before it can be attained.

Wisdom is part of a sequence of events associated with increasing our mental capacity and memory. It is located in the second stage of our human intellectual development; it is amid two other interrelated elements in which one's psychological and intellectual ability cannot be fully explored or utilized. To learn how to receive knowledge, you must first consider how it applies and relies on two other factors complementing it. That refers to the three foundations of intellectual development.

LEARNING: this is the first step towards cognitive and mental development. This is how increasing cognitive or intellectual growth begins; it is described as a deliberate attempt to acquire specific information on a topic or problem. Put data acquisition. Education is collecting, gaining, or learning knowledge or information. Therefore, each learning process results in the collection or acquiring of knowledge or information. All you'll ever get from learning is intelligence, which means information. That is, data is preserved and processed upon finishing the learning process. Therefore, the outcome of any education you go through is to gain knowledge on some topic or problem.

Knowledge ownership doesn't necessarily mean you're wise or clever, and it just means you're knowledgeable, and intelligence carrier. As the old saying goes, he who understands and doesn't understand what he does is no different than he who doesn't know or can't. This is why learning (knowledge) alone is not enough to achieve a high level of intellectual and mental ability. The need for action that gets us to the second stage of our path towards cognitive and mental development; the stage of doing or applying (wisdom).

DOING: this is where the first step of your path towards cognitive and mental development will be triggered. Because learning seeks to gain knowledge or information, the learned knowledge is typically in a dormant state waiting to be triggered. All you have experienced, either through reading, interpretation or experience, is equal to nothing unless it is done or used (applied). The importance of learning is not in gaining facts or expertise, but in its functional utility when applicable in real-time situations and circumstances. This is the source of wisdom, intelligence, and understanding added. To gain wisdom, one must first acquire knowledge or information by reading, only then can one enable what has been learned to receive the wisdom therein.

Wisdom consists in right-applied knowledge or information. Learning something by reading (knowledge) is quite different from knowing something by doing something (wisdom). All acts ' result is different. While it's true you can't have one without the other, and it's equally true that both yield two significantly different results. The do phase is very important to one's psychological and intellectual development because it is the ability to internalize and personalize what has been taught. The doing stage allows you to bring life into what was dormant, making you a creator rather than an information or knowledge holder. As we incorporate what we read, we are smarter as we obtain deeper insight from using the inactive iteration of knowledge or information gained into something more concrete and effective.

This is where knowledge or information is transformed from a dormant (passive) resource into a practical (active) resource. When we learn our goal shouldn't be to know, our goal must also be to use (apply) what we've known. That's how to receive knowledge. Why is knowledge so important to developmentally and intellectually? I cannot attain understanding without wisdom. Thus, in our journey towards mental or intellectual development, we reach the final process, understanding.

UNDERSTANDING: the interpretation of knowledge and experience to gain or grasp its meaning. Knowing is your understanding of the awareness, insight, and facts gained in a practical situation or scenario. It is rayed through your mindset. To understand better, reading (knowledge) and doing (wisdom) more will broaden your mindset. Understanding comes only when you've done what you've read. In other words, understanding comes only when you have to make use of what you've learned before. That is, only a wise person can achieve knowledge because knowing comes after you have learned.

KNOWLEDGE (learning); WISDOM (doing); UNDERSTANDING (interpretation). Training encourages us to know what to do, experience equips us to do, while learning helps us to perceive and puts into perspective what we have learned and achieved. Knowing is where we view and bring knowledge (what we learned) and understanding (what we did).

Chapter 5:
Types of Critical Thinking

The term "critical thinking" is actually incredibly broad.

Logical Reasoning

In its formal sense, logic is a system of rules according to which one may make inferences or draw conclusions. In other words, logic dictates how facts and conditions can be used to gain new understanding.

For example, if we begin with the factual statement that "A beagle is a type of dog," and then add the fact that "Rover is a beagle," we can then conclude, "Rover is a dog." However, if we are told, "Scruffy is a dog," the laws of logic do not allow us to conclude, "Scruffy is a beagle." All beagles are dogs, but it does not follow that any dog is a beagle, so we cannot say anything else about Scruffy.

Notice that the logical example above does not show evidence for any of its claims. The facts we started with (a.k.a. "premises") are true for the sake of argument. This is why critical thinking requires evidence as well as logic, to ensure that logical claims reflect reality.

Logic is an entire discipline in itself. For now, we'll cover the three types of logical reasoning that cover most arguments.

- Deductive reasoning or deduction guarantees the truth of a conclusion based on its premises.

All humans are mortal, and Andrew is a human. Therefore, Andrew is mortal.

It has been established that being human means being mortal, so if we know that Andrew is a human, then we know he is a mortal.

- Inductive reasoning shows something is probable but not definitely true according to its premises.

August has been the hottest month of the year in this region since we began tracking temperatures, so this year it will probably be the hottest month.

There is an established record of August being the hottest month during the year, so it is likely the hottest month of them all. Yet there is no scientific law or rule saying it has to be the hottest month, so it is possible that this year another month could be even hotter than August.

Notice that deductive reasoning starts with a general statement—in this case, a statement about all humans—and uses it to reach a specific conclusion, i.e., a conclusion about the specific case of Andrew. On the other hand, inductive uses a specific observation—in this case, what we know about August in the past—to make a general statement that is probable but not necessarily completely true, namely that August is the absolute hottest month of them all.

Scientific Reasoning

The scientific method is the process by which scientists and many other scholars and critical thinkers use tests and experimentation to support a claim. It is a general mode of thinking that—while primarily associated with experiments in the physical sciences such as biology, chemistry, and physics—is also prevalent in the social sciences as well as in philosophy and other disciplines.

The scientific method begins with a specific question, such as "How can I use electricity to power something?" or "Why are people suffering from this disease?" The person wishing to answer their question then provides a "hypothesis," an educated guess that they believe is possible based on what they know already. They will then conduct a test in the form of several experiments or the collection of data relevant to the problem.

They may experiment with different models for harnessing electricity, compare the health records and routines of the patients living in the infected region, or simply try different brands of detergent. They then analyze their findings to draw a conclusion.

Experiments are often replicated to test results under different conditions. For example, if the experimenter found a correlation between people suffering from the same diseases in a certain area and their ingestion of a chemical in the water, they might conduct an experiment on lab animals using those chemicals, or find another population demonstrating a similar correlation and analyze them.

No scientific theory is ever concluded to be one-hundred-percent accurate, and no experiment or test can demonstrate the absolute truth of any proposition. That is why scientists and others continue to test, experiment, and then reexamine things so that they can claim an overwhelming likelihood that their conclusion is correct. Evidence may never be perfect but imperfect evidence is not the same as a lack of evidence.

The Psychology of Critical Thinking

Critical thinking in psychology is defined as the habits and skills to engage in activity or exercise with reflection and criticism focusing on deciding what to believe and decisions to make. Critical thinking is a tool that is important even in psychology and it is being taught in psychology classes.

Many students coming to college have already formed theories and opinions of the subject and of life in general. When they are faced with college work, they get a shock when they find it is not what they thought it would be. Some students opt to cram the textbooks so that they will help them in the exams forgetting learning entails more than that.

For these reasons, psychology professors decided to teach critical thinking by approaching it in a systematic, purposeful, and developmental manner. The proposal was to teach critical thinking skills in 3 main domains of psychology: practical (the functionality), theoretical (development of scientific explanations for behaviors), and methodological (testing of scientific ideas).

Practical Domain

Practical critical thinking is expressed as the long-term goal of psychology teachers even as much as they don't spend a lot of time teaching critical skills to students in order to become better consumers or careful judges of character etc. Accurate interpretation of behavior is essential, but few teachers spend time teaching this to students and aiding them in understanding the way their thoughts are not invulnerable.

To instill critical thinking skills in students, encourage the practice of accurate description and behavior by giving students ambiguous tasks for example, as students to differentiate the behavior they observe from the inferences they find out of the behavior. With this exercise, students will discover that behavioral descriptions are consistent between observers, but inferences will vary widely. They realize that how they interpret is biased at times and personal because of their own preferences and values. Because of these strong differences in interpretations, students are likely to learn not to be overly confident about their immediate judgment or conclusions that they need to be more tolerant of ambiguity and be willing to give alternative interpretations as they need a good understanding of procedures in science, effective control skills and legitimate forms of evidence. With these, they will less likely be victims of multiple off-base claims or conclusions about behavior that faces us all.

Theoretical Domain

Theoretical critical thinking is about helping a student develop an appreciation of science in explaining behavior. This means that not only learning the content of psychology but how to organize psychology into concepts and why it is organized into concepts, theories, principles, and laws. Development of skills theoretically starts in the introductory class where the main critical thinking objective is applying and understanding concepts properly. For instance, when students are introduced to the principles of reinforcement, challenge them to find examples of the principles in the news or come up with stories that demonstrate the principles.

Mid-level courses require more advancement where students are moved from the application of concepts to learning how to apply theories. For example, provide a case study that is rich in abnormal psychology, and then ask students to interpret and make sense of it from different perspectives by making use of accepted and existing frameworks in psychology to explain behavior patterns.

In advanced levels, students can be asked to evaluate theory rejecting the least helpful or selecting the most useful. For instance, students can argue different models to discuss drug addiction in physiological psychology by evaluating the weaknesses and strengths of existing frameworks. They can choose the theories that work best by justifying their conclusions based on reason and evidence.

Graduate and honors courses go beyond the evaluation of theory and encourage students to create or come up with original theories. Students choose a difficult question on behavior and build their own theory-based explanations to the behavior.

This kind of challenge requires them to synthesize and include exiting theory as well as come up with new insights into the behavior.

Methodological Domain

Many departments give opportunities for students to build their methodological critical thinking skills by applying varied research methods in psychology. Beginner students first learn what the scientific method involves.

The next step will be applying their own understanding of the scientific method by identifying elements in existing research. For example, a detailed description of experimental design will help a student practice differentiating the dependent from the independent variable and understanding how researchers controlled for different explanations.

The next critical thinking in methodology goals includes evaluating the quality of existing research and critiquing the conclusions of the research findings.

Students may require encouragement from the teachers to overcome fear they sometimes experience for anything printed even their textbooks. Asking students to carry out a critical analysis on a sophisticated design may be too much for them to undertake.

They are likely to do much better when given assignments from bad designs so that they can cultivate critical abilities as well as the confidence to handle more complex designs. After this, students will be able to develop their own research designs in their methodology courses.

When you ask students to run their own independent research be it a comprehensive study on parental attitudes, a well-thought experiment on paired-associate studying or a study on the behavior of a museum patron, it makes students use their critical thinking skills and gives them an opportunity to practice with conventional writing in psychology.

After the students complete their work, ask them to evaluate the strengths and weaknesses of their work as this will help them in developing their critical thinking skills.

There are many ways and areas critical thinking and reasoning can be applied. Different disciplines and areas of life require the application of critical thinking processes in order to form the best decision and conclusions.

Four Goals for Critical Thinking

An adept critical thinker learns that the process requires a commitment to four goals each time it is used in order to get the most out of the endeavor.

Self-Direction

The first goal will be to strive for self-direction. Self-directed learning involves taking responsibility for your own acquisition and analysis of factual information from which you will learn. Your decision to dig deeper into ideas requires you to step out of your comfort zone, and you are going to have to make a decision about whether becoming a critical thinker is worth it to you. It is much easier to take things at face value – advertisers, marketers, politicians, and many others prefer that you not become a critical thinker, in fact! Most people are quite comfortable following cues from their highly conditioned subconscious mind and going about their days living in a world where they roll right along with the status quo and, quite frankly, lead mediocre lives.

Self-Discipline

The second goal as a critical thinker is does develop a strong sense of self-discipline. Learning and practicing critical thought is very challenging. Becoming a practicing critical thinker does not happen overnight and must be looked at as a process that takes a lot of introspection, self-analysis, and a commitment to change. In addition, if you have ever decided to learn a new skill and found it very difficult in the past, it is quite possible that you thought about giving up at some point because you found the work too hard. This is why so many New Year's resolutions are broken every year. As an example, one can visit a fitness center on January 2nd of any given year and usually find it to be very crowded and visit the same fitness center forty-five days later and see a marked difference in attendance. Self-discipline is not easy.

Self-Monitoring

The third goal for a critical thinker is self-monitoring. The biases and stereotypes we have taken on in our lives are a direct result of our experiences and the knowledge we have acquired from those experiences, as well as from what we have learned from those around us, and they may or not be accurate to some degree. Your mission as a critical thinker is to question your preconceived notions about your world and to assess and evaluate their level of accuracy as you move forward with your new ways of thought.

Self-Correction

The fourth goal a critical thinker must strive for is one of self-correction. This occurs when we reflect upon how we have perceived things in the past and then make decisions about the accuracy of those perceptions. This can be especially difficult because the knowledge base that resides in our subconscious has been hard-wired over the years. In order to have the self-discipline to correct erroneous thinking patterns (see how these goals work together?), we have to see the value of doing so. Critical thinkers will undoubtedly tell you that the benefit is that when you seek out and study various perspectives of issues; there is an opportunity for personal growth. They will also tell you, though, that questioning and correcting inaccurate perceptions that have been held throughout your life may cost you in terms of relationships. Not everyone around you will understand why you are suddenly questioning beliefs that they have held along with you for so long.

Chapter 5:
When to Apply Critical Thinking
to Improve Something

With such huge numbers of points of interest, it would appear we should think critically constantly. Albeit critical thinking is constantly helpful and can be applied all over the place, it's not functional to think along these lines constantly. It's about where you apply critical thinking as well as about when you apply it. A basic guideline to decide if you should utilize critical thinking in a given circumstance is the point at which the consequence of an issue, activity, objective, or condition (a head scratcher) is significant. Utilize critical thinking when the result has a significant effect on your business or individual circumstance.

For example, an easygoing email about where to have lunch, for the most part, isn't harmful if there's a miscommunication. However, a misjudged email about the necessities of a product, or a customer issue, may have broad ramifications. Thus, you should utilize a little critical thinking on the email that depicts a customer issue, instead of the email about lunch. Coming up next are three arrangements of examples of where and when you may utilize critical thinking. The first rundown contains significant level business works; the second, specific business issues or objectives; and the third, everyday exercises many uses to accomplish those business objectives. When you gain proficiency with the critical thinking tools, you'll add to this rundown with regions specific to your job.

Rundown 1: Business Functions That Benefit from Critical Thinking

- Record management
- Automation
- Budgeting
- Build versus purchase decisions
- Competitive examination
- Contracts
- Cost-decrease activities
- Crisis management
- Customer care improvement
- Customer maintenance techniques
- Development processes
- Diagnosis
- Employee authority improvement
- Employee productivity
- Financial decisions
- Human assets issues
- Information systems
- Inventory control
- Investment management

- Mergers and acquisitions
- New product thoughts and creation
- Operational productivity
- Outsource versus in-source decisions
- Partnership-related issues
- Product management
- Product showcasing
- Project management
- Proposal assessments
- Quality confirmation control
- Resource management
- Responses to demands for information (RFIs), demands for
- recommendations (RFPs), and offers
- Revenue age systems
- Risk management
- Sales and showcasing strategies
- Short-and long-haul business methodologies
- Space planning
- Succession planning
- Task coordination
- Technology framework
- Time, cost, and asset planning

Rundown 2: Examples of Specific Business Issues and Goals for Which Critical Thinking Should Be Used To comprehend a circumstance that is hazy:

- There is a whirlwind of action in deals, and the funnel line is at significant levels, yet brought deals to a close are level.
- Customer care call volume has greatly changed for no obvious explanation.
- An arrangement of assembling blunders has happened without clarification.
- Prospective customers appear to be keen on your product, yet few get it.
- The cost of activities is expanding, but the volumes being processed are not.
- A venture plan has achievements with specific dates and expectations, but people aren't meeting the time allotment cutoff times.
- A change in the standard has happened with no undeniable clarification.
- The measurements you're following are not able to do directing improvement or foreseeing a result.
- You've made a call for the main driver examination to discover the first reason for something, and it delivers a sudden outcome.
- Inventory or use of parts doesn't accommodate with the completed product.

- Delivered products or services don't accommodate with bills or income.

- Incremental costs in growth don't rise to decremental investment funds in decrease.

- Two people utilizing similar information get different conclusions.

- Conclusions about information don't make any sense or make sense.

- The diagram of something estimated or anticipated has an abrupt incline change.

- Customers are revealing a blunder rate that is significantly different from what you are estimating. To improve something:

- To decline the expense of customer care by 25 percent yet increment customer fulfillment.

- To increment productivity

- To improve correspondences between your specialization and another

- To decide how to change the advertising technique to be increasingly serious

- To develop your business

- To decline costs by 25 percent

- To find and contract progressively qualified applicants.

- To figure out how to manage ever-expanding social insurance costs.

- To abbreviate improvement times by a third.
- To decline mean time to fix (MTR) by 20 for every- penny
- To abbreviate request to-conveyance time significantly.
- To increment the quality of products so that the customer rating is 5 out of 5
- To improve promoting effort's outcomes
- When looking toward the future, consider:
- How would we be able to make another product that will contend with the new service our essential rival just presented?
- Two key representatives simply quit
- Our heritage product, which creates a larger part of our incomes and benefit, has a high steady loss rate. What is advisable for us to do?
- How do we keep away from this [insert unsavory event] from ever happening again?
- How do we duplicate what we simply accomplished for the following time?
- Should we fabricate or purchase our approach to grow our service contributions?
- How would we account for a development system?
- Given our financial limit, how would we achieve our destinations?
- How do I progress my vocation?

Rundown 3: Examples of Specific Day-to-Day Activities for Which Critical Thinking Can Be Helpful

- Assembling or fixing something
- Attending gatherings
- Assessing hazard
- Coaching
- Conducting brainstorming meetings
- Creating and interpreting overviews
- Creating introductions
- Engaging in financial planning exercises
- Engaging in one-on-one discussions
- Evaluating recommendations
- Making go or no-go decisions
- Organizing
- Planning your timetable/schedule
- Preparing talks
- Prioritizing
- Reading (Are you focusing on the fundamental importance of the words?)
- Reviewing contracts
- Reviewing spreadsheets
- Setting objectives
- Setting measurements

- Teaching (e-sends, headings, recommendations, reports, and so on.)

- Writing and directing execution assessments.

The Takeaway

Critical thinking can be applied wherever in your business and life but be specific. Utilize critical thinking when the result may have any kind of effect.

Reason why some people have a tough time with critical thinking

If you don't mind, comprehend that an enormous level of people can think critically. Sadly, this doesn't have any significant bearing, no matter how you look at it. Somebody may be a decent critical thinker in specific circumstances, but in other con messages, that individual can be a sloppy thinker.

That individual could be you. Likewise, a few people essentially don't think critically. Generally, this is a decision. This isn't something where people are only level out unequipped for critical thinking. Largely, they simply decide to think sloppily unexpectedly.

How Do People Struggle with Critical Thinking?

As referenced above, regularly, the setting assumes a job in whether an individual can think critically enough or not. Here are only probably the most well-known situations in which people battle to think critically.

They Think in Shallow. Some people look at the outside of an issue. They look and substance themselves with the most evident perspective on the issue. They don't look for subtlety. They don't look for special cases or potential logical inconsistencies. They simply bounce in with the two feet at the clearest introduction of an issue. As you presumably definitely know, because something looks self-evident, it doesn't imply that it is. Truth be told, as a rule, something that appears to be basic and clear is, in reality, exceptionally profound with a ton of moving parts.

This can have many outcomes and can trigger a chain response that can deliver a wide scope of results – the greater part of which are not too self-evident. The Jump to Conclusions Based Almost Purely on First Impressions It's terrible enough that many individuals tend to habitual sloppy thinkers that they just need to see certain facts for them to form a hasty opinion. As you most likely know, if you need to think of a conclusion that is both sound and legitimately informed and has a high prescient value, you need to look at all the facts. You can assemble them all. The issue is, people think that once they see a specific truth, they can hop to a conclusion because they can't suspend judgment. They feel that they're sitting around idly if they do. This truly spills out of the thinking of an "If I've seen one, I've seen all" sort of mindset. It likewise takes a lot of scholarly development and a reliable measure of emotional separation to try and attempt to look at the circumstance from a different point of view. It's effortless to be mentally lazy and simply look at the circumstance from your standard viewpoint.

It's Very Hard for Many People to Let Go of Biases and Prejudices

We were born into specific families, we were born into our time, and we live in one particular verifiable period. These significantly affect how we think, and they do shape how we look at the world. Overall, if we genuinely value reality and we need to think of judgments that depend dispassionately on facts, we need to relinquish these biases and prejudices. Our capacity to think critically and unbiased reach out past existence. These two components don't need to confine the quality of our judgments, essentially unreasonably. People are Just Simply Lazy Let's make one thing clear. Critical thinking necessitates that you look past the self-evident. It requires a tad of exertion. Many individuals think this is excessive.

Many individuals are under the feeling that they should simply think dependent on the vitality level that they are utilized to. Set forth plainly, if it requires an excess of mentally challenging work, people will prefer not to be annoyed. They'd preferably stick to what they think they know rather over upset their current casing of reference. They think that this is all the more trouble than it is worth. The long-standing thought of "opposites are drawn toward each other" is not scientifically legitimate.

If you look at the real research and proof, it isn't valid. However, this thought keeps on continuing, and we would all be able to thank sloppy and languid thinking for this.

A Lot of People are Mentally Uncomfortable with Critical Thinking

To take things to the following level, many individuals build up apathy about critical thinking because, at some level or another, they feel inconvenience. I realize it sounds somewhat outrageous to situate this as a "torment," but indeed, there is such an unbelievable marvel as mental torment. You need to understand that if you are attempting to make sense of something new or you're attempting to look at a circumstance with a crisp arrangement of eyes, it very well may be very excruciating because the "torment" exudes or originates from your personality splitting.

You need to put aside your sense of self. You need to conquer your pride. You need to push back or move back on your programming to look at circumstances from a crisp arrangement of eyes and impartially think of another conclusion. A great many people would prefer not to experience this because the moderate, careful exertion of defeating biases appears to be so wasteful. It seems as though it's not worth the trouble contrasted with simply hopping to a conclusion with the two feet. There's a considerable measure of emotional solace and accommodation included you do it at any rate.

You have to overcome the reasons above if you want to become a better critical thinker

If you don't mind, understand that whether or not you work in the scholarly world or not, or whether you work with any sort of systematic subjects or undertakings, you need critical thinking to be a progressively successful human being. The reason why there are such vast numbers of issues on the planet and the reason why there are such vast numbers of relationships that are not working to their fullest potential is that people are too anxious to even think about jumping to conclusions. People are too anxious to even think about thinking at shallow levels and in sloppy manners. This prompts a not exactly ideal quality of relationships, decisions, and life results. If you think you will find it settle on inappropriate decisions or if you think that there's a considerable amount of nervousness or lament in your life, or you're baffled at some level or another, you should turn into a progressively critical thinker.

You shouldn't have to see a psychologist. You probably won't need the assistance of antidepressants or antianxiety prescriptions. It might well turn out that a ton of your dissatisfactions is because of the way that you don't practice critical thinking at ideal levels.

How to Be a Critical Thinker Using These 7 Techniques

Every system has steps that you can follow. Some of them likewise have clinical examinations that help the legitimacy of every method. It will be ideal if you understand that the material underneath is proposed to fill in as a framework. Everybody's different. We, as a whole, originate from different backgrounds. We certainly have different arrangements of encounters. These differences, as little as they might be, largely, do include. This is the reason it's essential to remember that there is nothing of the sort as a type of enchantment projectile answer for sloppy thinking.

If you need to improve your critical thinking skills, utilize this framework, and tweak them depending on your understanding. By taking full close to home responsibility for strategies and tweaking them or modifying them to accommodate your everyday experience, you augment their value. You likewise improve the probability of joining these strategies into your everyday exercises. In the end, they become programmed. Why? They have become some portion of you.

Here are the seven procedures for improved critical thinking skills, in no specific request. While I propose that you give them each of them a shot, it's totally up to you regarding which system you start with. In any case, you need to utilize every one of them because they do have a scaling impact.

- Keep a receptive outlook.
- Develop and support your scholarly interest
- Learn to spot and oppose any interests to emotion
- Refuse to look at things at face value
- Make sure to stop and reflect when given things to think about consistently.

- Identify and conquer your negative self-talk or negative thoughts
- Be mindful of your present listening skills, and continually look to improve them

Chapter 6:
Best Practice for Improving
Critical Thinking Skills

There are many helpful ways to improve your critical thinking. Some of them are more labor-intensive than others, but they all can be done in a fairly short amount of time and don't require any special tools or designated space (though a pen and paper might be useful, depending on your own style).

Take A Breath, and Have a Thought

Begin to take even a moment before you answer a question, decide on a course of action, or make a decision. Train yourself to think carefully—even briefly—about what you are doing and why you are doing it. The world and people around us seem to move faster by the day but building critical thought into your everyday life can be revealing as well as productive.

Practice Careful Reading and Synthesis of Information

Does your reading ever become a blur? Do you find yourself thinking, "Get to the point" when you are in class? Try slowing down, focusing on each sentence, and seeing how all of those separate ideas form a larger point. Treat the comma, periods, and other punctuation marks in a sentence as actual stopping points for you to internalize what was just said.

Talk to Yourself

If you find yourself nodding or shaking your head at something said during a conversation or on the news, step back and consider why you made that gesture.

What are you agreeing or disagreeing with? Have you always felt that way? When was the last time you thought about the thing you are agreeing or disagreeing with as a topic of consideration—rather than something you simply agree or disagree with?

Break Down a Task into Its Parts

Critical thinking involves understanding a problem at its most basic level, including the different aspects of the issue or task. The next time you have something to do, try breaking it down into the different components that get you to your goal.

It could be as simple as needing to rake leaves:

1. Get the rake out.
2. Collect all the leaves into a pile.
3. Put all the leaves into a bag.

You now have three basic steps to rake the leaves. Is there any way you could rearrange or even shorten the process? For example, what if you combined steps two and three:

1.   Get the rake out.
2.   Collect all leaves into a bag as you rake them.

This is a very simple example, but it shows how even a simple task can be broken down, and perhaps improved on. Could you save time by just keeping the rake out in the yard?

Give Yourself a Real Goal

Do you watch too much television, or do you feel like you actually miss a lot of shows? You can ask the same questions about reading, exercising, or any other daily activity. Critical thinking can help you figure out a means of self-improvement.

First, ask yourself what "enough" or "a lot" looks like. If you watch ten hours of television per week and decide that it is too much, you just defined the terms of your problem. If you then say that you'd like to cut back to six hours of television per week, you just gave yourself a concrete goal—for example, a definite number rather than an abstract one (i.e., "less").

People spend millions of dollars on self-help books. While many of them are helpful and while different things work for different people, a common thread among many of these books is being honest and clear about your goals. Don't just plan to lose weight—plan to lose a certain amount of weight by a certain date. Determining that goal most likely requires input from your doctor or a weight loss professional, qualified people who can help you analyze the right goal. Again, this is just using facts from a trusted source and applying them to your problem using analysis and logic. It's critical thinking.

Know Thy Adversary

Critical thinking requires objectivity, the ability to separate yourself from emotions and question all assumptions. One good way to practice this skill is to analyze an opposing point of view or even advocate for it. Lawyers do this all the time—a lawyer does not necessarily always represent a person or side they agree with, but their job under the law is to give that side fair representation, which often requires the attorney to argue as though they actually were on that person's side. Lawyers are valued for their critical thinking for precisely this reason—their ability to separate fact from emotion and to make objective claims based strictly on evidence and logic.

Take an opposing viewpoint and consider:

• Why would someone take this side? Remember to be charitable to your opponent—assume, for the sake of this exercise, that they hold their own views for reasons as equally valid as your own, and not because they are ignorant, selfish, etc.

- Consider how this perspective might be beneficial. In your head or on paper, try to argue in favor of it. Can you set aside your own perspective, just for the sake of this exercise?

- Finally, try to argue against your own perspective from the other side. Formulate arguments that the other side may make against your side. This exercise can actually help you to strengthen your own side because you are now anticipating possible objectives as well as weeding out any contradictions or faulty points in your thinking.

The Martian Tourist

Why do you like the things you like? How did you come to like those things over other things? For example, why do you now love certain foods (or dislike others)? When was the first time you tried that food? Was there a pleasant memory associated with it? Have you been eating it for so long you can't even remember actually developing a taste for it? These questions aren't about justifying or explaining your taste in food, art, or other subjective areas, or ascertaining the best piece of music or kind of cuisine. Asking these questions allows you to look at personal preferences from a distance, to understand them and talk about them as something other than parts of you.

As an exercise, say you have a strange alien visitor come to Earth, and ask you to take them to your favorite pastime. Maybe it is watching television, going to a concert, or playing sports. Whatever the activity, this alien has never encountered it before and is not only unfamiliar with its rules or conventions, but it has no idea why any being would find it enjoyable. Try to explain why to them.

What do you enjoy about playing sports? Why would making yourself tired and sweaty be fun? What do the rules of the game add to it, and why are they necessary (as opposed to everyone just doing what they think is fun)? How does the experience of cooperating and competing with other humans add to the enjoyment of this activity?

To improve critical thinking skills is a lifelong study that is worth pursuing. Critical thinking is at the center of accumulation of knowledge and experience. After you have begun the practice of critical thinking, the question will be how to keep improving in critical thinking skills. What wisdom can be shared with learners that will help them keep their abilities just as well after their school years?

Teaching critical thinking skills does not require much in planning or equipment but just open and curious open-minds and some strategies. These are daily approaches designed to help you through the journey of enhancing and improving critical thinking skills so that they become an unconscious daily practice in a lifetime of learning.

Go through the strategies below carefully, internalize them, and begin to infuse them into your daily practices. Slowly, critical thinking will start becoming second to nature for you.

1. Do not waste time.

We all have had moments where we have wasted time and sadly realize that we cannot recover it back. Time wasted, unfortunately, can never be recovered. It is important to try and minimize the amount of time wasted on trivial things. For instance, instead of sitting in front of a TV set after work flicking through channels, you can spend that time reviewing how and when you practiced thinking throughout the day. Do this by asking yourself questions like these:

- What time did you do your worst thinking?

- When did you do your best thinking?

- What did you think about?

- If you were to repeat the day, what would you do differently?

- Were you able to figure out anything?

You can go through such question and even ask more spending as much time as you possibly can on them by analyzing your responses to the questions. The more practice you put on this, the more you will improve in your thinking patterns and habits.

2. Learn new things every day.

Make learning a lifelong habit. Learn something new every day. What have you always wanted to learn? Go for it. Keep learning until you find the answers that you are searching for regardless of the question you want answers for. Ignore what others may say but focus on gaining knowledge every day. Fulfilling an intellectual need is very important as well as developing curiosity habits to learn more.

It is never too late to learn new things nor is it very late to start new things. Look at history people who started fresh projects an age many people would think it is impossible. If you have ambitions for higher learning, don't get discouraged go for it. Learning has no boundaries—you are free to be curious in any field and learn.

Improving critical thinking skills isn't about your age. It is not about conquering the world—it is just learning a new skill that will help you in every aspect of your life. Believe in your potential and learn every day.

3. Have a questioning mind.

Since the beginning of time, the human mind has been curious about everything under the sun and even beyond the sun. In modern times, we encourage and teach our children to question, be curious, and explore possibilities. Questions are the essence of learning.

The ability to ask meaningful questions that will result in useful and constructive answers are at the core of critical thinking and a lifetime of learning.

Giving learning through leading questions as the focus ensures that both the learners and the providers do not just accept information presented to them, but they question it and search for different viewpoints because they don't take anything for granted. For instance, think of something that you heard and ask yourself some of the following questions:

- Who said it?
  o Is it someone you know?
  o Is the person in a position of power or authority?
  o Whoever told you this, does it matter?

- What was said?
  - o Did they provide opinions or facts?
  - o Did they provide all the necessary information?
  - o Did they leave out anything?

These questions among many others will help you make an informed decision because you will have applied the critical thinking process.

4. Practice listening actively.

There is this common expression that "many people are waiting for their chance to talk." This means no one is really listening. What do you understand by actively listening when someone is talking? Secondly, how are you able to listen actively to improve your critical thinking skills?

Studies have shown that people are inefficient listeners most of the time, that after listening to a presentation that is 10 minutes long, the average listener has understood and retained only 50 percent 48 hours after the presentation and it keeps dropping with the other participants.

Listening is not easy—it is hard work. Active listening requires even more work. Active listening means making conscious and purposeful effort to hear every word being said and most important, understanding the message being delivered. It also is about total comprehension of the speakers' intention—hence having empathy towards the speaker and information being passed. How then do you improve your active listening?

Just like any other communication skill, active listening can be learned, taught, and even practiced. The following tips will help you learn, improve, and practice active listening:

a) Talk Less – it is not possible to talk and listen at the same time. Hold on to responses and interruptions and be open by giving the person speaking the attention and whatever they need by you understanding what they are saying.

b) Adopt a listening mode – silence your environment and mind, open your mind to hear and feel comfortable as you listen. Ensure that you engage in eye contact.

c) Make the speaker feel comfortable – make a nod, utilize your body gestures, or do anything that will make the speaker realize you are listening and interested in what they have to say. Seating is also important for both the speaker and listener. Where is the speaker more comfortable? When you sit behind your desk or sit beside them? If a child, get at their eye level and avoid towering over them it is intimidating to them, and they may not be able to pass the information.

d) Remove distractions – this is about clearing the room of any physical things that may cause distractions, putting your phone on silent, switching off your TV or computer if they were on and may cause distractions. If the speaker requires privacy, ensure you give it to them by asking others in the room to excuse you, and then you close the door. This also gives the speaker the confidence that you will listen and understand all that they will be telling you and your response will be equally good.

e) Empathize – try and understand the situation from where the speaker is coming from. Put yourself in their position, ask necessary questions that will lead you to understand the speaker's position and feeling regarding the situation.

f) Don't fear silence – some people require time to form a response that is thoughtful. Don't rush them, and don't suggest what they should say. This hinders them from communicating honestly. Let them speak at their pace and understanding.

g) Put aside personal prejudice – this is also a very difficult thing to do because our experiences form who we are. To put all these experiences aside is a skill that requires help so as to be able to listen actively.

h) Heed their tone – be keen to understand the tone being used. Sometimes a tone may hide the meaning of a word and other times it may enhance the meaning. Be certain which tone it is so you understand what is being communicated.

i) Listen and identify the underlying meaning - most of the times you realize there is hidden meaning in some communication. Listen to understand or comprehension and secondly for ideas being communicated.

j) Put your attention also to the non-verbal communication – you can miss a lot of information if you are not keen on the non-verbal cues. People can communicate through body language and facial expressions—thus the reason that eye contact is necessary.

5. Solve the problem.

If there are so many problems and yet so little time to solve them, try to solve at least one. The problem will happen without our direct influence by action or choice, but they will not go away on their own. The secret lies in handling them one by one each day at a time and in learning the secret to avoiding them in the future.

Pick a problem a day and focus on finding a solution to it without dividing your attention. You may want to clear a long-held misunderstanding between yourself and another person, or are you getting very distracted at work? Alternatively, have you struggled with a project, and you want to improve it? Do you have anything in your house that needs fixing? Face the problem and find a solution. To help you solve the problem, here is an example:

Sample Process

This approach will give you a guideline for handling problems that you decide to face daily. The step by step guide will involve the following:

- Define and clearly state the problem as much as you can.
- Take time to study the problem and understand it and what is expected. If you have no control over a certain problem, set them aside and focus on the ones that you can find a solution for.

- Find out the information you need to solve the problem, actively gather all the necessary information to help you solve the problem.

- With keenness, interpret and analyze the information you have collected, pick reasonable and appropriate inferences that you can

- Find out what you can possibly do either shortly or in the long run. Make clear all your options for action and imagine the solution that seems ideal.

- Analyze your options, taking note of their pros and cons

- Adopt a systematic and strategic approach to the problem and go through with it.

- Observe the results of your action as they emerge and be ready to change your strategy if called upon to do so. Always be prepared to change your strategy, analysis or the statement of the problem and sometimes all the three as you gain more information that may drive to this.

The process of improving critical thinking takes practice and time. Hopefully, the above 5 practices or strategies will be useful to you in improving your critical thinking skills. With practice every day, you improve your skills and critical thinking becomes part of you.

Conclusion

By now, you will have realized the importance of critical thinking. This skill comes in handy not just in your professional life, but your personal life as well. Critical thinking promotes better decision making, and by making use of the strategies for better decision making that have been provided in this book, you will be able to take right decisions quickly. Goals are incredibly necessary if you want to achieve success.

Your brain is the super-computer that governs your life and body, and it's involved in everything that you do. Thinking logically doesn't mean that you don't have emotions.

Remember that your brain is unique, and it is more complex than any computer out there. It is an amazing organ, perhaps one of the most amazing in our bodies, and you need to take care of it and protect it from losing its elasticity and becoming complacent. So be sure to exercise your brain using the methods presented here and begin to think logically. It's going to be hard at first, but you're going to be able to do it if you stick with it!

Critical thinking is a lifelong skill. Every day we are learning something new or facing different challenges. These situations if we choose to look at them critically in order to draw the best conclusions, we continuously improve our critical thinking skills. It is possible to forget to apply critical thinking when analyzing the situation, but once you realize it, start again to ensure your judgment is the best based on the information you have.

Independence is a beautiful thing, and the better you get at critical thinking, the more you are going to become your own person. It is an odd thing, thinking that you are not your own person, but until you are able to take a hold of your life and think in your own functioning manner, you are not going to be independent.

You have a brain that works virtually like a supercomputer. It is that brain that directs the way your body functions, and it is the same brain that determines how you tailor your life. It also has a great influence on who you are as an individual, what you actually do and even the proficiency with which you do it.

.

with images of a happier life by the burgeoning self-help industry; not only do many bookshops now contain growing self-help sections, but there is also a rapidly increasing selection of websites, videos and smartphone apps that promise to help their users to find more happiness. Techniques such as meditation and mindfulness are also becoming increasingly popular, and their design and endorsement by academics and practicing psychological professionals lends support to their perceived effectiveness and success. A well-known example is Mindfulness-Based Cognitive Therapy, developed by Mark Williams, Professor of Cognitive Psychology at the University of Oxford. Books and courses devoted to it can be purchased by people who wish to find 'peace in a frantic world' (Williams and Penman, 2011).

Happiness and sociology: The odd couple

Despite its societal ubiquity, happiness, for many sociologists, has not been a popular area of inquiry, and as a result, it is rather under-researched across the discipline. This is despite its – albeit implicit – place in classical sociology; indeed, Weber writes about the ways in which life was shaped by religious ethics and the way people chose to live in order that otherworldly salvation was granted (Weber, 1904/2002). Similarly, Durkheim's work suggests that people seek happiness and well-being through a new moral order characterised by rituals and community (Durkheim, 1912/1961), and Marx's theory of alienation regarded workers in capitalist societies as being distinctly *un*happy as a result of alienation and an inability to realise their species-being (Marx and Engels, 1988). Nevertheless, few studies of happiness specifically exist as sociology has traditionally preoccupied itself with pathologies of society such as injustice, inequality, pain and suffering. In addition, happiness does not appear to sit well within any particular subfield of sociology; its place within the sociology of emotions, although important (as will be explored in Chapter 2), is not a wholly appropriate one, as happiness is not necessarily *just* an emotion, but also an aspect of personhood. By the same token, it is not fully welcome within the sociology of identity, due to its emotional characteristics.

Many of sociology's key theoretical underpinnings tend to be focused upon negative feeling, rather than on happiness, this is particularly the case with Marx and Engels (1988), who regard workers as being alienated, Weber, who asserts that we are trapped in an 'iron cage' of bureaucracy (1904/2002), and Simmel, who recognises that modern life is characterised by a loss of emotional vitality (1903). This may, in part, explain sociology's hostility to happiness scholarship. However, this also raises broader questions about the kind of relationship that critical sociology and social theory should have with the study of happiness. For Marxists and critical theorists, at least, happiness could be regarded as a naïve aspiration which is, in reality, an impossibility for most people living in an unequal, capitalist society. Nevertheless, as already highlighted, it occupies a central position in contemporary British society, and whether one understands it as a tool used by capitalists to maintain a false consciousness, or as a pleasant state that people should actively strive for, it is a goal that stands at the centre of many people's lives. Thus, if happiness is so important to people in this way, and is so central to the way in which society is governed and organised, then surely it should be a legitimate area for sociological investigation.

About this book

This book seeks to provide a sociological understanding of how people experience and perceive happiness. It does this by grounding an analysis of happiness within the first-hand accounts of 19 British adults, who were interviewed as part of an empirical study on which this book is based. These adults were asked a range of questions (see Appendix 1 for profiles of each respondent and Appendix 2 for a list of questions used in interviews). Their accounts, extracts of which are presented throughout the book, should not be seen as secondary to the analytic discussion; rather, the narratives of the interviewees are integral to this story and make up some of the most important aspects of the understanding of happiness that this book puts forward.

The book focuses specifically on the way in which people articulate their experiences and perceptions of happiness. Whilst it does this in a general sense, it also explores the ways in which interpersonal relationships, money and working life feature in people's understandings of happiness. This does not necessarily undermine the importance of other areas of life – such as health or religion – for happiness, but rather, they were chosen as a focus for the book as they were talked about in more detail by interviewees than other factors.